CONNECTIVE CLARITY

Art of Emailing

A Quick Guide to Effective Business Communications

Copyright © 2024 by Connective Clarity

All rights reserved. No part of this publication may be reproduced, stored or transmitted in any form or by any means, electronic, mechanical, photocopying, recording, scanning, or otherwise without written permission from the publisher. It is illegal to copy this book, post it to a website, or distribute it by any other means without permission.

Connective Clarity asserts the moral right to be identified as the author of this work.

Connective Clarity has no responsibility for the persistence or accuracy of URLs for external or third-party Internet Websites referred to in this publication and does not guarantee that any content on such Websites is, or will remain, accurate or appropriate.

Designations used by companies to distinguish their products are often claimed as trademarks. All brand names and product names used in this book and on its cover are trade names, service marks, trademarks and registered trademarks of their respective owners. The publishers and the book are not associated with any product or vendor mentioned in this book. None of the companies referenced within the book have endorsed the book.

First edition

This book was professionally typeset on Reedsy.
Find out more at reedsy.com

Contents

1. Introduction — 1
2. Email Tour — 3
3. The Anatomy of an Effective Email — 6
4. Mastering Your Inbox — 13
5. Email Etiquette Essentials — 21
6. Crafting Emails for Diverse Purposes — 29
7. The Art of Personal Touch in Professional Emails — 40
8. Overcoming Common Email Challenges — 45
9. The Future of Professional Emailing — 50
10. Conclusion — 56

1

Introduction

Have you ever stared at a blinking cursor on your screen, unsure how to begin an email that holds the key to your next big project? Or you've received a message that left you scratching your head, wondering what this person is really looking for you to do? Know that you are not alone. Emailing in the corporate world can be daunting, especially for those new to the game or those seeking to up their email game.

In this virtual and digital space, emails have become the lifeblood of our professional existence. They are more than just messages; they are the threads that weave the fabric of modern business communication. From conveying critical information to building relationships that can take you to the next level, emailing is a skill that transcends industries and positions. Yet, surprisingly, many find themselves lost in this vast sea of electronic correspondence, struggling to navigate its treacherous waters. We wrote this book to bridge the gap between the daunting expectations of people struggling to write corporate communications and their need for more guidance. Whether you are a fresh-faced intern, a recent graduate stepping into your first office, or a seasoned employee looking to sharpen your email-writing skills, this book is for you.

Now, picture this: no more agonizing moments spent wondering how to begin an email. No more asking questions, only to get more questions in return. Instead, envision yourself crafting emails that not only get the job done but also leave a lasting impression, emails that open doors and build bridges, emails that make you a true master of business communication.

In the following chapters, we will embark on a journey together, dissecting the art of emailing step by step. We'll dive into the anatomy of a well-structured email, unravel the secrets of subject lines that demand attention, and decode the subtle nuances of tone and etiquette. You will learn how to navigate the delicate dance of formal and informal communication, handle the dreaded reply-all debacle, and ensure your emails are crystal clear and concise.

But it doesn't stop there. We will also explore the psychology of effective communication, unlocking the power of empathy and active listening to enhance your email interactions. You'll discover the art of persuasion, crafting emails that inspire action and drive results. Throughout this journey, we will also sprinkle in real-life anecdotes and examples, making the learning experience informative and applicable.

This book isn't just about learning to write better emails but elevating your professional communication to new heights. Are you ready to embark on this adventure? Are you prepared to transform your email game and become a maestro of business communication? Buckle up, for the path ahead is both enlightening and empowering. Let's dive in and master the art of emailing together!

2

Email Tour

Welcome! In this chapter, we'll embark on a brief tour of the email landscape. If you're already a seasoned mailer acquainted with the landscape of an email application, feel free to skip ahead to the next chapter. However, if you're new to electronic correspondence or need a refresher, this is your pit stop to familiarize yourself with the essentials.

Folders

Imagine your email platform as a neatly organized filing cabinet, each folder serving as a labeled drawer that holds a specific type of correspondence. Here's a quick rundown of the essential folders you'll encounter:

Inbox: Your digital mailbox is where incoming emails land. It's where you find messages from colleagues, clients, and spam filters working overtime.

Sent or Sent Items: A record of your digital footprints. This folder stores copies of emails you've sent. Great for reference and tracking.

Draft: Think of this as your virtual sketchpad. It houses emails you've started but still need to send. It's handy for when inspiration strikes, but the timing isn't right to send.

Deleted: A digital trash bin. Deleted emails typically sit here until you empty the bin, or they automatically disappear after a set period. Think of it as a safety net for accidentally deleted messages.

Email Fields

Now, let's delve into the anatomy of an email. Think of it as a well-structured business letter but with a digital twist.

- *To:* The primary recipient(s) of your email. Enter their email addresses here. Use a semicolon or comma to separate multiple recipients.
  Cc (Carbon Copy): Stands for "Carbon Copy." This field is for recipients who should be aware of the email's contents but aren't the primary audience. It's like sending a copy to someone for informational purposes. (Similarly, you can also put the "Cc" names in the "To" field, and they will receive the email the same way.)
- *Bcc (Blind Carbon Copy):* Bcc stands for "Blind Carbon Copy." It allows you to send an email to multiple recipients without revealing their email addresses to each other, which helps maintain privacy and discretion. We will discuss specific use cases for Cc and Bcc in *Chapter 5 - Email Etiquette Essentials*.
- *Subject Line:* The email's headline. It's your chance to grab the recipient's attention and provide a glimpse of the email's content. Make it clear, concise, and enticing. *Chapter 3 - The Anatomy of an Effective Email* will provide tips on creating a good subject line.

Email Text Field

This field is where the magic happens. The body of your email is where you'll craft your message. Keep it organized, to the point, and free from spelling and grammatical errors. Composing in the body of the email will also be addressed in *Chapter 3*.

When considering the fields we discussed, view them as something other than mundane email elements. Instead, view them as tools that, when used effectively, can influence whether your email gets opened, read, and acted upon.

In the next chapter, we'll explore the art of crafting captivating subject lines and the nuances of effective email composition.

3

The Anatomy of an Effective Email

Welcome to the next chapter of our journey through the world of professional emailing. In the last chapter, we walked through the fields for your email; now, we'll work to populate that email text field correctly. Let's start with the basics of understanding the structure that holds our emails together.

Crafting the Perfect Subject Line

The subject line is the text that stands between your email and the recipient's attention. I think of it as the email's handshake: too weak and forgettable, too strong and off-putting. Your subject line should be firm, confident, and memorable, like a handshake. Crafting the perfect subject line balances clarity, brevity, personalization, and a keen sense of how to avoid the dreaded spam folder.

The clarity of your subject line is crucial—it should immediately tell the recipient what the email is about. This straightforward approach helps the recipient decide whether to open the email based on its relevance. Keeping your subject line under 50 characters is also essential because it ensures that the entire subject is visible in the recipient's inbox, preventing any critical information from being cut off.

Personalization adds a touch of warmth to this digital handshake and can significantly increase your email's open rate. Including a reference specific to the recipient makes the email more relevant and engaging. This simple step can make your message stand out among the flood of impersonal emails most people receive daily. It's like spotting a familiar face in a crowded room—immediately drawing your attention. However, it's vital to avoid words and punctuation that could trigger spam filters, such as "free," "guarantee," or excessive exclamation points.

In practice, crafting the email subject lines involves balancing informative and engaging content without triggering spam filters. "Meeting Rescheduled: New Date Inside" or "Feedback Requested: E-Book Draft Submission" are examples of subject lines that are clear, brief, personalized, and unlikely to end up in the spam folder. This approach ensures your emails get seen, opened, and read.

Salutations and Greetings: Starting on the Right Foot

If your subject line is like a handshake, your email's opening is the smile accompanying that handshake. It sets the tone for the entire virtual conversation. The formality of your greeting should reflect your existing relationship with the recipient. For initial contacts or those with whom you share a formal relationship, opt for traditional salutations such as "Dear Mr. Smith" or "Dear Professor Johnson." As your relationship with the recipient grows more informal, you can adjust your greetings to "Hi John" or "Hello Lisa," which are more relaxed. Also, personalizing the greeting by including the recipient's name makes your email more engaging. It shows that you have taken the time to address them directly, fostering a connection quickly.

Being culturally sensitive in your choice of greeting is also essential, as norms vary significantly across cultures. What's considered polite in one culture may be too casual or even rude in another. For instance, in some cultures, using a person's first name too soon is frowned upon. Doing some research to understand these nuances can show respect and foster a positive rapport with your recipient. If that information is unknown or when in doubt, err on the side of formality. Why? Openers such as "To whom it may concern" may seem like a safe bet for unknown recipients; it can come across as impersonal and disengaged. If you need clarification on the recipient's name, try to find it out. If that's not possible, a specific title or department can help, such as "Dear Hiring Manager" or "Hello Customer Service Team," indicating that the message is crafted with their collective identity in mind.

By choosing the proper salutation and greeting, you display professionalism and add a personal touch to your emails, creating a conducive environment for effective and pleasant communication. This careful consideration at the outset encourages a positive response and lays the groundwork for successful email exchanges.

The Art of Conciseness: Writing Emails that Get to the Point

In email communication, conciseness is not just a stylistic choice; it's a form of consideration. Every word in your email demands a slice of the recipient's time, so ensuring each one earns its keep is crucial. Writing concise emails is about respecting the recipient's time by making your message as brief as possible without sacrificing clarity or essential details.

Firstly, prioritize clarity in every line. Before sending an email, review each sentence to ensure it directly contributes to the message you're trying to convey. If a sentence doesn't add new information or clarify a point, it's likely a candidate for removal. For instance, instead of writing, "I am writing to inform you that we have decided to move the meeting scheduled for next Monday to the following Wednesday due to some scheduling conflicts that have arisen," say, "The meeting is moving to Wednesday due to scheduling conflicts."

Using bullet points is another effective way to distill your message into digestible pieces. This format breaks the information into manageable chunks and highlights the key points, making it easier for the recipient to grasp the essentials quickly. For example, if you're summarizing a report, instead of embedding the critical findings in paragraphs, list them as bullet points:

- Total sales increased by 15%.
- Customer satisfaction scores rose to 4.8/5.
- A new product line will launch next quarter.

Also, avoid jargon and complex language as much as possible. Your goal should be to communicate, not to confuse. Opt for simple, straightforward language that anyone can easily understand, regardless of how familiar someone is with the subject. For instance, instead of saying, "We anticipate a fortuitous augmentation in our consumer base subsequent to the implementation of the proposed marketing stratagem," say, "We expect more customers after starting our new marketing strategy."

Finally, keep your paragraphs short and focused. Large blocks of text can be overwhelming and may discourage the recipient from reading the entire message. Aim for paragraphs no more than three or four sentences long, each addressing a single idea. This approach enhances readability and helps recipients quickly find the information they need.

By embracing the art of conciseness, you respect the recipient's time and ensure that your messages are clear, direct, and easy to act upon. This approach makes your emails more effective and increases the likelihood that they'll receive the attention and response they deserve.

The Power of Closing Statements: Leaving a Lasting Impression

Just as the opening of your email sets the tone, the closing statement leaves an enduring impression— often what people remember most. A robust and thoughtful closing can reinforce your message, prompt action, and even solidify a relationship, all with a few well-chosen words.

All closings should conclude with a clear call to action (CTA). Be explicit about what you want the recipient to do next. This direction helps avoid ambiguity and encourages the desired outcome. For example, instead of vaguely ending with "Let me know your thoughts," you could say, "Please reply with your feedback by Thursday."

Next, express gratitude. A simple "Thank you for your time" or "I appreciate your help" acknowledges the recipient's effort and makes your message more positively received. It's a small gesture that can significantly impact how your email is perceived and enhance the rapport between you and the recipient.

Offering additional assistance is another critical element of your closing statement. Phrases like "If you have any questions, feel free to reach out" show your willingness to provide further support and encourage ongoing communication. It signals that you're not just ending a conversation but can help if needed and engage further.

Finally, choosing the proper sign-off is crucial for leaving a lasting impression. Your sign-off should match the tone of your email and your relationship with the recipient. For formal emails, "Best regards" or "Sincerely" are appropriate, while "Best" or "Cheers" can be used for more casual correspondence. The sign-off is your final touch, so make it count.

The power of a closing statement lies in its ability to reinforce your message, prompt action, and strengthen relationships. By crafting your closing with a clear call to action, expressing gratitude, offering further assistance, and selecting an appropriate sign-off, you can ensure that your email conveys your message effectively and leaves a positive, lasting impression on the recipient.

Looking back at this chapter, it's clear that effective emails require attention in several key areas: creating engaging subject lines, choosing the proper greeting, ensuring content is clear and to the point, and ending with a strong closing statement. This chapter has provided a practical toolkit for improving your emails, focusing on the essentials that make your messages readable, memorable, and impactful. Applying these techniques can enhance your ability to communicate effectively via email, fostering better relationships and encouraging more positive responses. Remember these principles as you compose each email, recognizing that each email is an opportunity to make an impression—so make sure it's lasting.

4

Mastering Your Inbox

In today's digital age, email has become a pivotal communication tool in professional settings and in our personal lives. However, with the convenience of email comes the challenge of managing an ever-growing influx of messages, leading many to feel overwhelmed and stressed by their cluttered inboxes. With each ping, notification, and unread message count, it may feel like we answered one email only for three more to appear. Chapter 4 aims to transform your relationship with your email inbox, turning it from a source of endless distraction into a well-oiled machine that enhances your productivity and peace of mind. From achieving the coveted state of Inbox Zero to implementing advanced automation techniques, this chapter provides the strategies and tools to master your inbox efficiently. Let's embark on this journey to email enlightenment, starting with the cornerstone of inbox management: achieving and maintaining Inbox Zero.

Inbox Zero: Achieving and Maintaining an Organized Inbox

The pursuit of Inbox Zero is less about obsessively clearing every message and more about mastering the flow of your digital correspondence. It's a philosophy where your inbox doesn't command your day; instead, you wield control over it with precision and purpose. Here are a few tips:

- Adopt a clear-cut strategy for each email: if it's unnecessary for future reference, delete it immediately; otherwise, archive it for later. This simple yet effective approach keeps unnecessary clutter at bay.
- Audit your subscription lists by unsubscribing from newsletters, promotional emails, or updates that no longer provide value or relevance to you. This action alone can drastically decrease the amount of incoming mail.
- Avoid the constant interruption of email notifications and carve out specific times dedicated solely to managing your inbox, such as the beginning, midday, and end of your workday. This approach helps maintain focus on your tasks and allows for more efficient email handling. Constantly checking emails can fragment your attention and hamper productivity.
- Implement the two-minute rule for quick decision-making: If an email requires a brief response or action you can complete in two minutes or less, do it immediately. For more time-consuming emails, schedule a specific time to deal with them, preventing them from lingering and contributing to clutter. We will discuss prioritizing in the upcoming section.
- Additionally, use the organizational tools and filters available in your email client. These can automatically sort incoming emails according to set criteria, such as sender or subject, reducing the time

you spend manually organizing your inbox.

As you can see, achieving Inbox Zero is realistic and can significantly reduce stress and improve productivity. By integrating these strategies, maintaining your inbox moves from a source of stress to a streamlined hub of productivity and focus.

Effective Use of Email Folders and Tags for Organization

Implementing an organized system using email folders and tags from the outset is a strategic move that can save you time and hassle later. This approach allows for swift retrieval of essential emails and keeps your inbox manageable, regardless of size.

By setting up a logical folder structure that reflects the different facets of your work or personal life, such as projects, clients, or specific types of communications like invoices or individual messages, you create an intuitive framework for managing your emails. This structure enables quick filing and easy retrieval, streamlining your email management process. Using tags or labels also allows for flexible organization, enabling emails to be categorized across multiple dimensions—for example, by project, urgency, or required action. This multi-tagging approach facilitates efficient email retrieval across various categories without duplicating messages in several folders.

It's also crucial to periodically review and adjust your organizational system to align with your changing projects, priorities, and roles. An effective folder system is dynamic and evolving. For instance, if you find the "Read Later" tag overflowing with emails you never actually read later, it might be time to reconsider how you prioritize information. Similarly, you might discover that emails related to a specific client are more manageable if subdivided into more specific folders, like "Invoices" and "Project Plans."

Furthermore, leveraging your email client's capability to automate the sorting process through rules or filters can dramatically reduce your time on manual organization. For example, suppose your inbox sees an email from a specific recipient. In that case, it can automatically place it into the "Client Feedback" folder and perhaps tag it as "Needs Reply" if the subject line includes a question mark indicating an inquiry. This way, important emails are presorted, allowing you to focus on content rather than organization. You ensure your inbox stays organized with minimal effort by automatically directing incoming emails to designated folders or applying specific tags based on predefined criteria like sender or keywords.

In essence, by initially investing time to create and periodically refine a tailored system of folders and tags—and utilizing rules for automatic sorting—you can transform your inbox into a highly efficient workspace. This organized approach makes managing your daily email flow easier and ensures no message goes unnoticed or unaddressed, streamlining your communication process and enhancing overall productivity.

Prioritizing Emails: Techniques for Efficient Processing

Now that your inbox has a clear structure of folders and tags, the next crucial step is mastering the art of prioritizing your emails. This step is vital to ensure that you respond to emails as they come in and address them in an order that aligns with your priorities and responsibilities. Let's explore some techniques for efficient email processing that will help you prioritize effectively.

First, adopt a system of email triage. Email triage is the step after the two-minute rule referenced in the first section. Once you quickly scan your emails and decide on their importance and urgency, you can use markers such as flags, stars, or custom labels to categorize emails. For instance, an email that requires immediate action or response can have a red flag, while important but non-urgent emails can have a different color.

Understanding and respecting your priorities is also crucial in this process. It involves recognizing which emails align with your most immediate tasks and which contribute to your longer-term goals. This discernment lets you decide which emails to open and respond to first and which can wait.

Employing the urgency and importance matrix is another effective strategy. This method involves categorizing emails into four quadrants— urgent and important, important but not urgent, urgent but not important, and neither— you can focus on emails that are both urgent and important first while scheduling time later for those that are important but not urgent. This method helps you manage your time and attention efficiently and ensure critical emails aren't lost.

Finally, beware of false urgencies. It's common for emails to be marked as urgent to grab your attention, but not all require immediate action. Developing the ability to distinguish between genuinely urgent emails and those that can wait is essential. Trust your judgment and understanding of your priorities to guide you. This skill will prevent you from getting sidetracked by less important tasks and maintain your focus on what truly matters.

Applying these techniques to prioritize your emails ensures that your attention focuses on the most critical communications. This approach helps you stay on top of your most pressing emails and prevents less important messages from monopolizing your time and attention.

Automating Routine Emails: Saving Time with Templates

In the quest to master your inbox, the goal of working smarter, not harder, should be your guiding principle. This mantra is especially true when it comes to handling routine emails. Automating responses to common inquiries or situations saves you significant time and ensures consistency and professionalism in your communications.

An excellent place to start is by identifying the types of responses you frequently need and creating templates for these scenarios. The templates could range from standard informational replies to updates or responses to common service inquiries. Having these templates at your disposal means you can quickly tailor and send out responses without starting from scratch each time, saving precious moments and ensuring consistency across your communications. For instance, imagine you frequently receive emails requesting pricing information. Instead of typing out a response each time, you could have a template named "Pricing Info Response" ready. With a few clicks, you can customize and send this template, ensuring a swift reply without the effort of crafting a new email each time. Employing a mail merge tool can be incredibly effective for communications that need to go out to multiple individuals, such as newsletters or event invites. Merge tools let you personalize elements like greetings in each email, making recipients feel valued while streamlining your process.

Auto-responders are another vital tool in your automation arsenal, perfect for the most commonly asked questions or requests you receive. By automatically providing recipients with FAQs, basic information, or expected timelines for a response, you can enhance customer experience and free up your focus for more demanding tasks. Auto-responders are also great in scenarios like vacation periods, like, "Thanks for your email. I'm out of the office with limited access to email. For immediate assistance, please contact [Alternative Contact]." This message keeps everyone informed and redirects urgent matters appropriately, ensuring everything runs smoothly in your absence.

Lastly, exploring the comprehensive range of email automation tools available can further refine your workflow. These tools offer functionalities like scheduling emails to be sent at optimal times, automating follow-up based on recipient actions, and more, ensuring you remain proactive in your communications without the manual burden. An excellent example would be scheduling a series of follow-up emails after a client meeting. The first follow-up could be a thank-you email sent the day after the meeting, the second a check-in email a week later to discuss any further questions, and perhaps a third email two weeks later offering additional resources or assistance. These scheduled emails ensure consistent, thoughtful communication with minimal manual input once set up.

Incorporating these automation techniques into your routine email handling elevates your productivity and upholds a high communication standard. By investing a little time in setting up these systems, you reclaim much more in the long run, allowing you to concentrate on the aspects of your work that genuinely require your personal touch and expertise.

We just walked through effective strategies for transforming your inbox from a source of endless distraction into a streamlined conduit for effective communication. Through the methods outlined in this chapter—from achieving Inbox Zero and organizing with folders and tags to prioritizing emails, automating routine responses, and managing high volumes—you're equipped with a comprehensive toolkit for mastering your inbox. These practices enhance your productivity and contribute to a more organized digital life, allowing you to navigate your email with confidence and ease. By consistently applying these techniques, you ensure that your inbox serves you, supporting your goals and freeing you to focus on the work that matters most. Embrace these strategies as part of your daily routine to maintain control over your digital communications and turn your inbox into an ally in your professional and personal success.

5

Email Etiquette Essentials

Professional communication is crucial for success and requires more than just sending and receiving messages. Email is the pivotal thread that weaves together your networks of collaborators, peers, and other essential contacts. Yet, to truly harness email's power, you must understand its etiquette and rules. This chapter will focus on the critical aspects of email etiquette that professionals must master to enhance their email interactions. Rules such as understanding when and how to use Cc and Bcc to keep the right people in the loop without compromising privacy, the best practices for handling email attachments to avoid common pitfalls, crafting a concise and informative email signature that reflects your professional identity and making informed decisions about using the "Reply All" function to avoid unnecessary email clutter. This chapter will improve your emails and contribute to more productive and respectful professional relationships by providing practical advice and clear guidelines.

Understanding Cc/Bcc: Strategic Use in Professional Emails

Understanding the strategic use of Cc (carbon copy) and Bcc (blind carbon copy) is crucial in professional emails to inform relevant parties, protect privacy, and maintain clarity in email interactions.

When you Cc someone on an email, you want to keep them in the loop even though they are not the primary recipient. For example, if you send a project update to a client or supervisor, you might also Cc a colleague working on the project to keep your coworkers informed without requiring any action from them. It says, "This information is relevant to you, but no response is needed." Also, as a courtesy, explain why someone is Cc'd in your actual email when needed. For example, "Adding John to Cc as he'll be taking over this project next week" provides clarity and context to all parties involved.

Bcc is slightly different and should be used for privacy when sending a message to multiple recipients. For instance, if you're sending a company-wide memo but want to keep everyone's email addresses private, you would place all the recipients in the Bcc field. This way, you avoid sharing personal contact details with the entire group, respecting everyone's privacy.

However, it's essential to use Cc and Bcc judiciously. Overusing Cc can lead to information overload for people who might not need to be involved in every conversation. Similarly, using Bcc too often can lead to a lack of transparency and collaboration since team members will not know who received the email. Used wisely, Cc and Bcc can be valuable tools for managing your email communications.

The Dos and Don'ts of Email Attachments

Attachments via email are crucial tools for sharing documents, images, and other files. However, to ensure these attachments are courteous and practical, it is vital to follow certain etiquette guidelines.

The Dos

- Check File Sizes: Before attaching files, consider their size. Large files can be cumbersome for recipients, possibly exceeding their inbox limits or leading to long download times. For files over a few megabytes, consider using cloud storage services like Google Drive or Dropbox and provide a link to the file instead. This practice will ensure recipients can access it without inconvenience.
- Mention Attachments in the Body: It's easy for recipients to overlook attachments. Always mention in your email's body that you've included an attachment, such as "Please find the attached report for your review." This statement not only alerts the recipient to the attachment but also reinforces its relevance to your message.
- Use Universally Accessible Formats: To avoid compatibility issues, use file formats that are widely accessible. PDFs are ideal for documents because they preserve formatting across different platforms. Most companies and clients use Microsoft Office for spreadsheets or presentations. If not, consider sharing a Google Drive link, which allows recipients to view the file without needing specific software.
- Scan for Malware: Before sending any attachment, ensure it's free from viruses or malware. Even unintentionally sending an infected file can harm the recipient's system and erode trust. Use reliable antivirus software to scan files before attaching them to your emails.

The Don'ts

- Don't Send Unnecessary Attachments: Be selective about what you attach to your emails. Including too many attachments or files not directly relevant to your message can overwhelm recipients and dilute the focus of your communication. Stick to including only those necessary attachments for the recipient to understand or act on your message.
- Never Assume Privacy: When sending sensitive or confidential documents as attachments, such as Personally Identifiable Information (PII) or Protected Health Information (PHI), never assume they're completely secure. Use encryption for highly sensitive documents or consider secure document-sharing services that require authentication for access.
- Remember to Follow Up: If your email includes a necessary attachment requiring action, such as a form to complete or a document to sign, it's good practice to follow up with the recipient if you have yet to receive a response within a reasonable time frame.

By adhering to these simple rules, you navigate the complexities of email attachments, ensuring your communications remain professional, secure, and considerate of your recipient's needs and constraints.

Email Signature: Your Professional Digital Footprint

Your email signature is your professional digital footprint in email communication, serving as a sign-off and representing your professional identity. It's the equivalent of a business card, subtly conveying your professionalism, brand identity, and how someone can contact you outside of email. Crafting an effective email signature requires balancing providing essential information and maintaining simplicity and readability. Most companies have signature templates approved by upper management and HR. If not, follow these tips to ensure you get the most out of your signature.

Any successful signature must include the basics: your full name, job title, company name, and contact information. These elements are non-negotiable for a professional signature, as they provide the recipient with immediate context about who you are and how they can respond to you beyond email, whether through a direct call or by visiting your company's website.

Adding social media links to your signature can be beneficial, but it's important to be selective. Never include personal profiles from Facebook or Instagram, for example, if they do not pertain to your business persona. Only include professionally relevant profiles that contribute positively to your professional image, such as your LinkedIn profile. Adding your LinkedIn extends the network of your professional presence and offers recipients a way to learn more about your professional background and achievements.

Consistency with your company's branding is crucial. If your company has a specific color scheme, font, and logo, incorporating these into your email signature reinforces brand identity and contributes to a cohesive professional image. Although they can enhance your signature's visual appeal, be cautious of having too many graphics with logos or images. They can increase email loading times and be blocked or appear differently on various email clients. If you choose to include a graphic, ensure it's small, optimized for web use, and adds value to your signature.

Lastly, keep your signature concise. A signature that's too long can distract from the message of your email and may only display partially on mobile devices. Aim for an informative but streamlined signature, ensuring it complements your email rather than overpowering it.

Overall, your email signature is critical to your professional online presence. It encapsulates your identity and offers vital information in a compact format. By balancing essential details with a clean, brand-consistent design, you can create an effective email signature that is a powerful tool in your professional communication arsenal.

Navigating Reply All: When and How to Use It

Using "Reply All" properly in email communication will prevent you from becoming a source of frustration among colleagues and contacts. While useful in certain contexts, this feature can easily lead to cluttered inboxes and unnecessary distractions if not used appropriately. Understanding when and how to use "Reply All" can significantly improve email etiquette and efficiency within any professional setting.

"Reply All" should be used sparingly. Before clicking it, consider whether your response is relevant to all original recipients. The feature is particularly appropriate in discussions where group collaboration or consensus is required, and everyone needs to be in the loop. For example, in a project planning email where input from several team members is necessary, "Reply All" ensures everyone can access the same information and contribute to the conversation. However, a common misuse would be to "Reply All" to express enthusiasm about a company-wide event and inquire about bringing a guest. Now, everyone's inbox is flooded with responses to these questions, followed by others chiming in with their thoughts and queries about the event. This cascade of "Reply All" messages not only clutters inboxes but also diverts attention away from more pressing work matters. It creates an unnecessary distraction for employees who may not be directly involved in the event's planning or have specific questions about it.

That said, consider the implications of your response on all recipients' inboxes before using "Reply All." Ask yourself if the information you're about to send is necessary for everyone to know. If the answer is no, it's better to reply only to the sender or select individuals who need that information. Unnecessary "Reply All" responses can lead to information overload and dilute the importance of messages requiring collective attention.

If you're ever unsure whether "Reply All" is appropriate, it's prudent to seek permission from the original sender or a primary recipient. A quick check can prevent potential over-communication while respecting others' preferences and inbox management strategies.

When used correctly, "Reply All" is a powerful feature that can facilitate efficient group communication. By applying these considerations—using the feature sparingly, assessing the relevance of your response to all recipients, and seeking permission when in doubt—you can navigate "Reply All" effectively, contributing to a more streamlined and respectful email culture.

Mastering the essentials of email etiquette is more than just a skill; it's a necessary practice in maintaining professionalism and clarity in digital communication. By thoughtfully managing Cc/Bcc fields, attaching files appropriately, designing a concise email signature, and using "Reply

All" wisely, you elevate the quality and efficacy of your emails. These practices do more than streamline your inbox; they cultivate a culture of respect and efficiency within your professional network. Adhering to these email etiquette essentials showcases your commitment to clear and respectful communication. It ensures your emails contribute positively to your workplace's communication landscape, reinforcing your professional reputation with each message sent.

6

Crafting Emails for Diverse Purposes

The multifaceted world of email communication requires a keen understanding of each message's specific purpose. Crafting Emails for Diverse Purposes delves into the art and strategy behind tailoring your emails to make lasting impressions, persuade effectively, offer sincere apologies, and provide constructive feedback. This chapter offers a roadmap to mastering these varied forms of communication, emphasizing the importance of adapting your approach to fit the context of each interaction. From personalizing introductions to engaging in persuasive tactics, expressing regrets professionally, and delivering feedback tactfully, you'll learn how to harness the power of email to achieve your communication goals. Each section will equip you with the tools and insights needed to confidently navigate the email landscape, ensuring your messages are impactful and resonate with your intended audience.

Introduction Emails: Making a Memorable First Impression

Introducing yourself to someone new via email can be daunting, but it doesn't have to be. Introduction emails are your first step towards establishing a connection and making a memorable first impression. The key to these emails is personalization. Personalization demonstrates to the recipient that you've taken the time to understand who they are and what they do. This initial effort sets the tone for the relationship, indicating respect and genuine interest.

When personalizing your greeting, go beyond the generic "Dear [Name]" by mentioning something specific you admire about their work or achievements. For example, "Dear Dr. Smith, I was truly impressed by your latest publication on renewable energy solutions…" This approach shows that you've done your homework and are purposefully reaching out.

Clearly stating your intention in the introduction is also essential. Be upfront about why you're contacting the recipient and what you're hoping to achieve. Whether it's seeking advice, proposing a collaboration, or simply expressing a desire to connect over shared interests, clarity helps the recipient understand the purpose of your email. For example, suppose you're hoping to collaborate on a project. A clear statement like "I'm reaching out to discuss a potential collaboration on [XYZ topic]" immediately informs the recipient of your intent and why they specifically are being contacted.

Keeping your introduction concise and engaging is key to holding the recipient's attention. Respect their time by getting straight to the point, but do so in a way that sparks interest. A short but compelling introduction, such as "I was moved by your work with [XYZ topic] and feel there's a synergy between our projects that could spark interesting outcomes," is more likely to get a response than a lengthy, general overview of your background.

Finally, including a specific call to action is crucial. Suggest a straightforward course of action instead of leaving the next step ambiguous. Whether it's a request for a meeting or a phone call, guiding the recipient on how to proceed makes it easier for them to engage in a way that is beneficial to you. Instead of ending with a vague "I look forward to hearing from you," propose something concrete like, "Would you be available for a brief call next Thursday to explore this idea further?" This message shows initiative and makes it easy for them to say yes by providing a clear next step for them to follow.

A memorable introduction email involves a blend of personalization, clarity of purpose, brevity, engagement, and a clear call to action. By carefully considering these elements, you can make a solid first impression that lays the groundwork for a fruitful outcome.

Writing Persuasive Emails: The Power of Persuasion

In everyone's professional life, there will come a time when you will need to convince someone that your way is the best. Writing persuasive emails involves a delicate interplay of credibility, emotion, and logic— a trio that, when balanced correctly, can significantly enhance the persuasiveness of your message. This section explores how to weave these elements into your email communications to convince your audience effectively.

Immediately establishing your credibility lays a trustworthy foundation for your message. For example, when recommending a new software solution, you might start with, "In my time here dealing with [XYZ topic], I've seen firsthand the challenges we face. Based on this experience, I've identified a solution..." This message asserts your authority and reassures the recipient of your capability to propose a valuable recommendation.

Next, tap into the recipient's emotions to create a connection beyond mere facts. Painting a vivid picture of how your proposal benefits the recipient personally or professionally can be powerful. "Imagine the impact we can have on [XYZ topic] by launching this program and simplifying the work of everyone involved." Such language helps the recipient visualize the positive outcomes, making your proposal more compelling.

Supporting your persuasion with data, facts, and a clear, logical explanation helps to strengthen your case and solidify your argument. Including statistics from a reputable source provides concrete evidence to support your case. For instance, a statement like, "Studies from other clients using this system have shown a 25% increase in [XYZ topic] compared to their previous setup." This data appeals to logic and provides a solid rationale for considering your proposal.

The final puzzle piece is concluding your email with a clear and actionable call to action. Rather than leaving your request open-ended, guide your recipient toward the next step: "Could we discuss this proposal further in our next team meeting? Your insights would be invaluable." Specifying what you're asking for makes it easier for the recipient to engage further, increasing the chances of a positive outcome.

By strategically combining credibility, emotion, and logic within your persuasive emails and wrapping up with a direct call to action, you create a compelling narrative that enhances the likelihood of your message resonating with your audience and eliciting the desired response. This balanced approach ensures that your emails are read, felt, and acted upon.

Feedback and Critique: Delivering Constructively

Feedback and critique are instrumental in the success and growth of every person in a business environment. Because of their importance, delivering feedback and critique via email requires a thoughtful approach to ensure your message is constructive, actionable, and received in the intended spirit. The goal is to foster growth and improvement rather than diminish or discourage. Here's how to craft feedback that is both effective and respectful.

Start by framing your feedback with positive observations to set a supportive tone and make the recipient more receptive to your critique. For instance, if you provide feedback on a presentation, you could begin with, "Your deep dive into the [XYZ topic] was insightful and added great value to the discussion." Highlighting strengths first helps balance the critique that follows and shows that your overall view is balanced.

Be specific about the areas that need improvement. Vague comments can lead to confusion and make it difficult for the recipient to act on your feedback. Instead of saying, "Some of your data was wrong and needs to be updated," pinpoint the exact areas for enhancement, such as, "Your data about [XYZ topic] was outdated and new information is available."

Detailed and specific points help the recipient understand what changes are needed.

Offer actionable suggestions rather than just pointing out what was lacking. For example, if the issue was a lack of data, suggest specific sources or data to include. "The updated information can be found [location], which also incorporates new industry surveys and case studies relating to the data." This statement points out the gap and provides clear direction for addressing it.

Encourage dialogue by inviting the recipient to discuss the feedback further. For example, "I'd be happy to discuss how to find the information and ways to update the presentation together." Offering your support for their development and improvement emphasizes that the purpose of your feedback is constructive, fostering an environment of collaboration and growth.

Constructive feedback and critique involve starting with positive observations, being specific about areas for improvement, offering actionable suggestions, and encouraging further dialogue. Adhering to these principles ensures that your feedback is heard, appreciated, and acted upon, contributing positively to the recipient's professional development and the overall work environment.

Apology Emails: Expressing Sincere Regret Professionally

It has happened to the best of us. You made a mistake and need to admit it, fix the problem quickly, and move forward. Although it seems daunting at the time, acknowledging errors and offering sincere apologies through email can maintain and even strengthen business relationships. Creating an apology email requires a careful approach, where direct acknowledgment of the mistake and taking full responsibility are paramount.

Begin your email by openly acknowledging the error without delay or obfuscation. For instance, if you missed a deadline, start with, "I realize that I failed to meet the deadline for our project deliverable..." This straightforward admission demonstrates honesty and responsibility from the outset.

Expressing genuine regret helps the recipient understand the impact of your mistake. Your apology should reflect a sincere understanding of how your actions (or inactions) affected the project or relationship. For example, "I understand this has put our timeline at risk and may have caused additional workload for you and the team. I deeply regret any stress or inconvenience this has caused."

Following your acknowledgment and expression of regret, offering a tangible solution or remedy to the situation is important to show your commitment to making amends and preventing similar issues in the future. For example, "To rectify this, I am prioritizing the completion of the deliverable and expect to have it to you by the end of the day tomorrow. Additionally, I am reviewing the project plan to prevent delays like this moving forward."

As you conclude your email, reaffirm your commitment to high standards and quality in your work to restore faith in your professional capabilities and signal your dedication to continuous improvement. For instance, "I take full responsibility for this oversight and am committed to upholding the highest standards in our future projects to ensure this does not happen again."

An effective apology email involves more than just saying sorry; it requires a genuine acknowledgment of the mistake, expressing sincere regret, offering a practical solution, and reaffirming your commitment to excellence. Handling apologies with care and professionalism can turn a potentially harmful situation into an opportunity to demonstrate integrity, accountability, and a solid commitment to everyone involved.

The Role of Empathy in Email Communication

Connecting and seeing the world from another person's perspective is the greatest gift we humans can offer one another. Empathy, or stepping into someone's shoes, understanding their point of view, and conveying your message in a way that resonates with their feelings and circumstances, acts as a bridge that connects you to the recipient on a deeper level.

If you know the recipient is experiencing a difficult situation, start by acknowledging any challenges or concerns they might face. For example, they're going through a busy period. In that case, you might begin your email with, "I understand this is a hectic time for you..." to show you recognize and respect their situation, setting a considerate tone for the rest of your message.

Also, adjust your tone based on the recipient's current state. If they're celebrating a success, your tone should be congratulatory and upbeat. Conversely, a more subdued and supportive tone would be appropriate for dealing with a setback. For instance, after a successful project launch, you might write, "Congratulations on the successful launch! Your hard work has truly paid off." If the project faced challenges, a message like, "I know this project presented some unexpected hurdles. Your perseverance is admirable," would be more fitting.

Another way of demonstrating empathy is offering your support or assistance where relevant. It could be as simple as saying, "If there's anything I can do to support you during this time, please let me know." This statement shows empathy and reinforces your willingness to help. Avoid generic phrases that might come across as insincere or formulaic. Instead, tailor your message to reflect a fundamental understanding of the recipient's situation. For example, "I was so sorry to hear about the challenges you've encountered with the project. It's a lot to manage, and I'm here to help however I can."

Empathy is more than words; it's about forging a connection that acknowledges the person's humanity. By understanding and reflecting on their perspective, adjusting your tone accordingly, offering support, and ensuring your expressions of empathy are genuine, you can create meaningful, impactful email interactions that resonate on a personal level.

Crisis Communication: Email Strategies for Difficult Times

Similar to other types of emails some view as stressful (introductions or giving feedback, for example), there will come a time when you will need to address a crisis. Navigating crisis communication via email demands swift action, transparency, and a deep sense of empathy, all underscored by a calm and reassuring tone. The initial step in effective crisis management is promptly communicating with stakeholders, whether clients, employees, or partners. An early acknowledgment of the issue, such as, "We are aware of [the crisis] and are actively working to understand its implications," can prevent misinformation from spreading, demonstrating your commitment to openness and transparency.

As the situation develops and more information becomes available, conveying the news transparently and actionably is crucial. It provides clear instructions or details about what is happening, what it means for the recipient, and any steps they need to take. For example, in a cybersecurity incident, an email might outline specific actions users need to secure their accounts, thus offering practical advice amidst uncertainty.

Empathy plays a critical role in crisis communication, acknowledging the emotional and practical challenges that recipients may face due to the crisis. Phrases like, "We understand the concerns this may raise and sincerely apologize for any stress caused" resonate on a personal level, showing that your organization cares about more than just the logistical aspects of the crisis.

Also, for an email like this to be successful, maintaining a calm and reassuring tone throughout your crisis communication will help alleviate anxiety and demonstrate that your organization is handling the situation with competence and poise. Even amid a crisis, a professional and composed email can instill confidence in recipients, assuring them that steps are in progress to resolve the issue effectively. For instance, a statement like, "Please rest assured that we are taking comprehensive measures to address [the issue] and are committed to keeping you informed every step of the way," can provide much-needed reassurance during turbulent times.

By blending promptness, clarity, empathy, and a calm demeanor in your emails, you craft communications that not only address the crisis at hand but also maintain and potentially enhance trust in your organization. This balanced approach to email communication during difficult times ensures that you manage not just the crisis but also the invaluable relationships with those affected by it.

Crafting emails for diverse purposes is an invaluable skill in the professional toolkit, enabling clear, effective, and respectful communication across several contexts. This chapter is a comprehensive guide to navigating various emails with finesse and effectiveness. Professionals can navigate their digital correspondence with confidence and precision by understanding the nuanced demands of introduction, persuasion, feedback, apology, empathy, and crisis management emails. This chapter has equipped readers with the strategies to tailor their emails for specific purposes, ensuring they leave a positive, lasting impression on their recipients. By applying these tailored techniques, professionals enhance their ability to communicate effectively and foster stronger relationships, contribute to a more positive workplace culture, and achieve tremendous success in their collaborative endeavors.

7

The Art of Personal Touch in Professional Emails

These days, emails often serve as the primary mode of business communication - covering everything from straightforward transactions to complex negotiations. The challenge lies not in just conveying information but conveying it with a personal touch that resonates with your recipient. This chapter explores the balance between maintaining professional decorum and infusing your emails with elements that reflect your personality and attentiveness to the recipient's needs and context. These techniques transform standard exchanges into meaningful interactions, fostering stronger relationships and enhancing communication effectiveness. Through practical tips and strategic insights, this section will guide you on personalizing your professional emails to captivate your audience, making your messages memorable and impactful amidst the daily influx of digital correspondence we must wade through.

Beyond Templates: Injecting Personality into Emails

Since most business interactions lack a face-to-face component, incorporating personality into your emails transforms them from mere transactions to engaging, memorable communications. When appropriate, begin by referencing details from previous interactions. Statements like, "I hope the conference in [Location] last week offered you new insights," demonstrate attentiveness and foster the sense of an ongoing conversation. Remember, personalization is key! Tailoring messages to acknowledge the recipient's recent achievements or current endeavors, like "Congratulations on your team's recent performance award—truly well deserved!" makes the email feel thoughtfully crafted just for them.

When thinking about the recipient, striking the right balance between professionalism and personalization is crucial; weaving in personal touches makes your emails more relatable and engaging. You can strike that balance by expressing genuine enthusiasm for a project that aligns with your mission and personal interests, for example, "I'm genuinely excited about the possibility of working together on this project—it echoes both our teams' shared commitment to [XYZ goal]." These strategies enrich your emails with personality and cultivate deeper professional relationships, making every email an opportunity to connect, engage, and create more fruitful collaborations.

Using Humor Wisely in Emails

"A sense of humor is part of the art of leadership, of getting along with people, of getting things done." – Dwight D. Eisenhower

Using humor in email is another way to let your personality show through. When used correctly, humor can lighten the mood and enhance relationships. However, use humor wisely to ensure it lands appropriately. Understanding your audience is the first step; what resonates with one person might fall flat or offend another. Consider the recipient's culture, age, and the nature of your professional relationship. For example, a quip about needing a gallon of coffee to get through Monday might be well-received in a casual update to your team but could seem out of place in a formal proposal to a prospective client.

Keeping the humor light and relevant is also vital. It should complement the message rather than distract from it. For instance, when announcing a team milestone, a humorous remark about the journey ("We've come a long way from our humble beginnings powered by instant coffee and late-night brainstorming!") can celebrate the achievement while keeping the tone upbeat.

Beware of sensitive topics such as politics, religion, or personal matters. Humor in these areas is highly subjective and can easily misinterpreted, potentially damaging professional relationships. If you're unsure about a joke or humorous comment, testing it with a few colleagues can offer valuable insights into how a wider audience might receive it. This small step can prevent potential misunderstandings and ensure your attempt at humor positively influences your email's impact.

When used wisely, humor can add a layer of warmth and personality to professional emails, making them more enjoyable and memorable. However, it requires a nuanced understanding of your audience and the context of your message. By adhering to these guidelines, you can effectively incorporate humor into your emails, enhancing your communications with fun that strengthens connections without compromising professionalism.

The Psychology of Email Responses: Encouraging Engagement

Leveraging psychological triggers in email communication can significantly enhance engagement and prompt responses. Understanding and applying these principles can turn your emails from being read to being acted upon. Here's how to effectively incorporate psychological triggers to encourage engagement from your recipients.

Creating a sense of urgency or scarcity is a powerful motivator. Phrases such as "Only a few slots left for our webinar" or "Please reply by the end of the day Thursday to secure your spot" can compel recipients to act quickly to avoid missing out. However, ensure these claims are genuine to maintain trust and integrity in your communications.

Incorporating social proof into your emails can also increase engagement by building trust and credibility. For instance, including a true customer testimonial lends credibility to your message and can influence recipients to join the crowd. This tactic leverages the human tendency to follow the actions of others, especially in decision-making scenarios with positive outcomes.

The principle of reciprocity is another effective trigger; by offering something of value, you naturally encourage the recipient to respond in kind. The exchange could be helpful advice, a valuable resource, or exclusive content. For instance, sharing a free e-book on a relevant topic and inviting feedback or questions can encourage more engaged responses.

Personalizing the call to action (CTA) based on the recipient's interests or past behaviors can also boost response rates. Tailoring your CTA to reflect the recipient's specific situation or previous interactions with you makes it more relevant and compelling. A personalized CTA like "Given your interest in [XYZ topic], I thought you might want to be part of our upcoming webinar on [XYZ topic]" speaks directly to the recipient's known interests.

You can craft messages that capture attention and inspire action by skillfully leveraging these psychological principles in your email strategy. This approach ensures your emails serve as effective conduits for engagement, fostering a more dynamic and responsive communication channel with your audience.

Mastering the art of personal touch in professional emails is essential for transcending digital communication barriers and forging genuine connections. Emails can become powerful tools for building relationships, encouraging engagement, and effectively conveying messages by integrating personalization, humor, and understanding psychological triggers. Personalization ensures that each email reaches the inbox and resonates with the recipient on a human level, making communication more meaningful and impactful. As we navigate the complexities of professional interactions in the digital age, remembering the value of a personal touch can transform our emails from mere text to memorable exchanges that enhance understanding, cooperation, and rapport.

8

Overcoming Common Email Challenges

Chapter 8 delves into the intricate world of email communication, unraveling the common challenges that professionals face daily. This chapter will equip you with practical strategies to navigate ambiguous messages, prevent and manage miscommunications, and tackle the growing concern of email-induced anxiety. Through practical advice and actionable tips, this chapter is your guide to overcoming these obstacles with confidence and ease.

The Curse of Ambiguous Emails: How to Ask for Clarification

Ambiguous emails can create confusion, leaving recipients puzzled and unsure how to proceed. Yet, with a tactful approach, seeking clarity becomes a straightforward process, using a blend of directness, organization, and courtesy. For instance, if an email about a project update leaves you uncertain about your role, initiate your clarification request with gratitude and precision: "Thank you for the detailed update on the project. I'm eager to contribute effectively but need some specifics to proceed. Could you clarify which sections of the report I should focus on for our upcoming presentation?"

If your confusion spans multiple points, itemizing these in bullet form can simplify the process for you and the sender, providing an easy template for them to answer direct questions. "To ensure I fully grasp our next steps, I'm looking to understand the following:

- Who is the lead presenter for the presentation?
- What is the expected format for our project outline?
- When is the deadline for the project submission?"

Sometimes, though, the complexities of an email's content may be too convoluted for another round of emails to solve. In scenarios like that, proposing a brief call or meeting can save time and prevent further confusion. A suggestion would be, "There's a lot to unpack here. Would you be open to a quick call or meeting this afternoon to go over these points?" Always round off your request with a note of thanks, acknowledging the extra effort on the sender's part to clarify any confusion: "I appreciate you taking the time to guide me through these questions. Thank you in advance for your insights."

By being direct yet polite, organizing your questions for clarity, suggesting a call for complex issues, and expressing gratitude, you can easily navigate the confusion and ensure you have all the necessary information to move forward. These strategies transform potential email confusion into more transparent, more concise communication.

Preventing and Managing Email Miscommunications

If unchecked, email miscommunications can derail projects and wreak havoc on due dates and timelines. Proactively preventing and managing these miscommunications are essential to completing any successful assignment. A key tactic is starting each email with an explicit statement of purpose, setting the stage for clear understanding. For instance, if you're beginning a new project phase, start with, "The purpose of this email is to outline the next steps for project X as we transition into phase two." A statement like that sets the context for the recipient about the details that follow.

It's equally important to foster a culture of feedback, encourage questions, and offer thorough explanations as needed. Encourage open dialogue by inviting your recipients to seek clarification on any points that are unclear. This two-way communication channel ensures misunderstandings are caught early, thereby establishing a reciprocal dialogue for clarity. For instance, "Please let me know if any part of the project outline needs further explanation."

Another crucial habit often overlooked is re-reading your email through the recipient's eyes before sending it. This reflective practice helps identify potential misinterpretations or tone issues, allowing for adjustments that preempt misunderstandings. Adjusting your email to remove such ambiguities can prevent confusion before they occur.

Despite these precautions, should miscommunications occur, addressing them directly and as soon as possible is best. Acknowledge any confusion and provide clear, concise information to rectify the issue. For example, if an email about a deadline caused some confusion, follow up with, "I realize my previous email may have been unclear. For clarification, the final submission date is [specific date]." Addressing the sticking point can quickly resolve confusion and realign team efforts. Adopting these practices significantly reduces the likelihood of email miscommunications and ensures the resolution is quick when they occur.

Email Anxiety: Coping Strategies for Email-Induced Stress

As helpful as email is to our everyday lives, it still has the potential to become overwhelming. Email-induced stress, or email anxiety—a common yet often overlooked phenomenon—can significantly impact productivity and overall well-being. As we navigate endless streams of information and correspondence, developing strategies to manage email-induced stress is crucial for maintaining a healthy work-life balance. Awareness is the first step towards management. Recognize stress signs—such as feeling overwhelmed by an overflowing inbox or experiencing dread at the thought of opening your email application. Acknowledging these feelings as a common response to stress is the first step to developing healthy coping mechanisms. Those mechanisms include the strategies mentioned in *Chapter 4 - Mastering Your Inbox*, such as inbox organization and email prioritization.

Also, learn to be easy on yourself and set realistic expectations. You may find that not every day ends with an empty inbox, and that's perfectly acceptable. Understand that productivity isn't solely measured by how efficiently you manage your emails.

When you do begin to experience signs of stress, incorporate mindfulness techniques such as deep breathing to center yourself. For those who find the anxiety too burdensome, seeking support from colleagues, mentors, or mental health professionals is helpful. Sharing experiences and strategies with others can provide new insights and lessen the impact of work on your stress levels.

By adopting a mindful approach to email, accepting that perfection is unattainable, and understanding when to seek help, professionals can ensure that email remains a valuable tool rather than a source of constant stress, thereby preserving productivity and peace of mind.

9

The Future of Professional Emailing

As we stand on the brink of new advancements in digital communication, Chapter 9, "The Future of Professional Emailing," ventures into the evolving landscape of email in the professional world. This chapter explores the dynamic shifts anticipated in email etiquette, the profound impact of remote work on email communication, the blending of email with social media, and the exciting possibilities ushered in by the next generation of email technology. As professional emailing adapts to technological innovations, changing workplace norms, and the global expansion of professional networks, understanding these trends and preparing for them becomes essential. Through insightful analysis and forward-looking strategies, this chapter aims to equip you with the knowledge to navigate the future of emailing effectively. Embracing these changes will enhance the efficiency and impact of our emails and ensure that we remain at the forefront of digital professionalism in an increasingly interconnected world.

Anticipating the Evolution of Email Etiquette

As the professional landscape continues to evolve, so does the etiquette surrounding email communication. The nuances of etiquette are constantly shifting, necessitating awareness and adaptability to stay aligned with contemporary standards. As the workplace becomes increasingly diverse, professionals from various generations and cultures will each bring their communication preferences and expectations to the table. For instance, while baby boomers might appreciate more formal email structures, Millennial and Gen Z professionals may lean towards a more casual tone, valuing brevity and directness. This diversity underscores the importance of an adaptable communication style, where one might need to switch from a formal, detailed email when engaging with senior executives or older colleagues to a more concise, straight-to-the-point message for younger colleagues or clients.

Furthermore, with globalization at its peak, understanding global email etiquette has never been more crucial. Professional interactions now span continents, making it essential to be mindful of and sensitive to the email communication styles prevalent in different cultures. For example, professionals in Japan might value politeness and formality in their emails, while those in Australia might prefer a more relaxed approach. Keeping abreast of these evolving trends and preferences requires regular research and a willingness to adapt, ensuring your email communications are respectful, professional, empathetic, and culturally informed. As we anticipate the future of email etiquette, the key lies in balancing these diverse expectations, ensuring that our emails reflect not just our personal or organizational brand but also respect the shifting dynamics of the professional landscape.

Email and the Remote Work Revolution

The remote work revolution has dramatically shifted communication dynamics, with emails becoming the linchpin that holds spread-out teams together. As organizations adapt to teams dispersed across various locations and time zones, the role of email in ensuring clear, concise, and effective communication has never been more critical. For example, if a project manager in New York has to coordinate with team members in London, Toronto, and Sydney, they would rely heavily on email to set tasks, communicate deadlines, and share updates. This scenario highlights the necessity for clear and concise emails while also considering each team member's different working hours and cultural nuances.

Regular updates and check-ins via email will help reinforce the presence of remote team members by making their contributions visible and appreciated. For instance, circulating a succinct, well-crafted weekly email highlighting project milestones, individual accomplishments, and upcoming objectives can make team members feel connected and valued, regardless of their physical location. Also, balancing synchronous (real-time) and asynchronous communication becomes essential in a remote work setting. Emails are ideal for non-urgent, detailed communications that allow recipients to respond at their convenience and don't require immediate feedback. However, knowing when to switch to real-time communication tools like instant messaging or virtual meetings for urgent discussions or brainstorming sessions will help maintain a project's momentum. Through strategic, mindful email communication, remote teams can navigate distance challenges, ensuring productivity and collaboration remain at their peak.

The Convergence of Email and Social Media in Professional Communication

The convergence of email and social media in professional communication represents a significant shift in how we establish and nurture professional relationships today. This blend offers a multifaceted approach to networking, personal branding, and information sharing by leveraging the strengths of each platform to facilitate deeper connections. For instance, including links to your LinkedIn profile in your email signature invites recipients to engage with your professional persona beyond the confines of the email. This connection enhances your brand and provides a richer context of your professional background and interests.

Social media insights can further personalize and inform email communication. Imagine analyzing a contact's LinkedIn activities to understand their professional interests and recent achievements. You can incorporate this information into your email communication, such as congratulating them on a recent promotion or referencing a thought-provoking article they shared, making your emails more relevant and engaging.

Furthermore, the strategy of engaging contacts across both email and social media platforms can strengthen professional relationships. For example, after initial email exchanges, continuing the conversation on LinkedIn can add a dynamic layer to the interaction, making it more informal and continuous. This cross-platform engagement ensures that professional relationships mature more holistically.

Additionally, email campaigns that promote participation in professional social media activities, like webinars hosted on LinkedIn or industry discussions on Twitter, exemplify how email can catalyze social media engagement. Professionals can effectively bridge the gap between email and social media interaction by inviting email recipients to join these platforms for specific events or discussions. This convergence broadens the scope of professional communication and opens new avenues for collaboration and knowledge sharing in today's digitally interconnected world.

Preparing for the Next Generation of Email Technology

As we stand on the precipice of the next wave of digital transformation, preparing for the future of email technology is paramount for anyone aiming to stay at the forefront of efficient and impactful communication. Integrating new technologies promises to redefine how we manage, personalize, and interact with our emails. For instance, adopting AI-driven tools can significantly streamline email management, enabling more intelligent sorting, automatic prioritization, and even predictive typing to save time and enhance productivity. Imagine an AI assistant that drafts responses based on your writing style and schedules them for the most practical times, optimizing your engagement rates. These types of automation technologies will revolutionize personalization in email communication by tailoring messages to each recipient's specific interests, behaviors, and needs. The technology could automate personalized email follow-ups after a webinar, suggesting resources aligned with each attendee's engagement during the event.

The future also holds advancements in email interactivity, moving beyond static text to dynamic, engaging content directly within emails. For example, embedded forms for instant feedback, interactive infographics, or real-time content updates could significantly increase engagement and collect valuable insights without ever leaving the inbox.

However, with these technological advancements comes an increased responsibility for privacy and data protection. As email becomes more integrated with other business tools and platforms, ensuring the security of sensitive information remains a top priority. Professionals must stay informed about the best email security practices, such as end-to-end encryption or multi-factor authentication, to protect against data breaches and maintain trust in digital communication.

Embracing the next generation of email technology means more than just keeping up with the latest tools; it involves a proactive approach to understanding how these innovations can enhance communication strategies, improve efficiency, and secure data. By anticipating these changes and adapting accordingly, professionals can leverage email technology to its full potential.

The journey ahead in adapting to evolving email etiquette, embracing the remote work revolution, integrating social media, and preparing for new email technologies is exciting and chock-full of possibilities. This chapter has illuminated the path forward, highlighting the need for clarity, adaptability, and a keen awareness of the changing digital landscape. By staying informed, open to change, and proactive in adopting new practices and technologies, you can not only keep pace with the future of emailing but also harness its full potential to enhance your ability to connect, understand, and collaborate. As we move forward, let this exploration serve as both a guide and an inspiration, empowering you to navigate the future of email communication with confidence and skill.

10

Conclusion

Mastering email communication is a pivotal skill in the tapestry of professional interaction, transcending simple writing ability to embody the essence of connection, engagement, and influence. This book has journeyed through the multifaceted world of email, underscoring that success in this domain relies on what we say and how we say it, ensuring our messages are clear, concise, and courteous. These principles form the backbone of effective email interactions, guiding us to not only send messages but also to truly connect.

In today's global marketplace, we must recognize the role of cultural sensitivity and the ability to adapt one's communication style to respect different norms and preferences. Understanding these differences is crucial for building and maintaining effective international and cross-cultural relationships. Furthermore, the strategies for managing an inundated inbox—prioritizing emails, embracing automation, and striving for efficiency—highlight the significance of organization in maintaining productivity and sanity in a world flooded with digital correspondence.

CONCLUSION

As we travel the ever-evolving landscape of email communication, the call for continued learning and adaptation becomes loud and clear. Staying abreast of emerging practices, technologies, and etiquette ensures our continued effectiveness and relevance along with the changing times. This book encourages not just passive reading but active practice and application of its principles. Much like any other skill, proficiency in email communication is honed through consistent practice, and each interaction presents an opportunity to apply and refine these techniques.

Let this book serve as both a guide and an inspiration, pushing you to master the multifaceted art of email communication. You have the insights and strategies necessary to adeptly navigate the complexities of professional emailing. But the journey doesn't end here; I invite you to share your experiences, challenges, and successes in applying these principles with coworkers and peers. Together, we can foster a community dedicated to continuous learning and improvement, elevating our collective email communication skills to new heights.

www.ingramcontent.com/pod-product-compliance
Lightning Source LLC
Chambersburg PA
CBHW051535240526
45471CB00020B/2822